Let' Gold

by Ainslie Mitchell

Harcourt
SCHOOL PUBLISHERS

Cover ©Photodisc; 3 ©Photodisc; 4 ©Stephen Barnham/Goldfields Historical and Arts Society, Dunolly; 5 ©Photodisc; 6 ©Photolibrary.com; 7 ©Australian Picture Library/Corbis; 8–9 ©Photolibrary.com; 10 ©N.A.S.A; 11 ©Photodisc; 12–14 ©Photolibrary.com.

Printed in China

ISBN 10: 0-15-350661-X
ISBN 13: 978-0-15-350661-1

Ordering Options
ISBN 10: 0-15-350599-0 (Grade 2 On-Level Collection)
ISBN 13: 978-0-15-350599-7 (Grade 2 On-Level Collection)
ISBN 10: 0-15-357842-4 (package of 5)
ISBN 13: 978-0-15-357842-7 (package of 5)

4 5 6 7 8 9 10   0940   15 14 13 12 11 10 09

Many valuable things can be found in the earth's crust. There are precious stones and metals. One of the metals is gold.

Gold is rare. It is often found in very small flakes. It can also be found in lumps called nuggets. The biggest nugget ever found weighed more than 125 pounds (about 57 kg). That's as much as about two second-graders!

The biggest collection of gold in the world is stored at the Bank of New York. The gold there is owned by many different countries. The Bank of New York is a very safe place to keep gold. It is worth billions of dollars.

Around 6,000 years ago, the
ancient Egyptians learned how to mine
and use gold. They separated the gold
from the rock found in the hills by the
Red Sea.

Gold became very important to
the Egyptians. They used it to make
art and jewelry. Many ancient gold
objects have been found in the famous
pyramids in Egypt.

Gold can last a long time. It never rusts or rots. Beautiful gold objects are sometimes found in the ground or in the sea thousands of years after they were buried. When the objects are discovered, they are still perfect.

Gold is easy to work with. It is a soft metal, so it can easily be made into different shapes. It can be bent or rolled or twisted without breaking.

A small piece of gold can be beaten into a large sheet or pulled into a long wire. It can be made harder by mixing it with other metals.

Gold can be used for all kinds
of things. Sometimes gold is used
in making cloth. It is common to use
gold in electronic equipment, such as
computers and telephones.

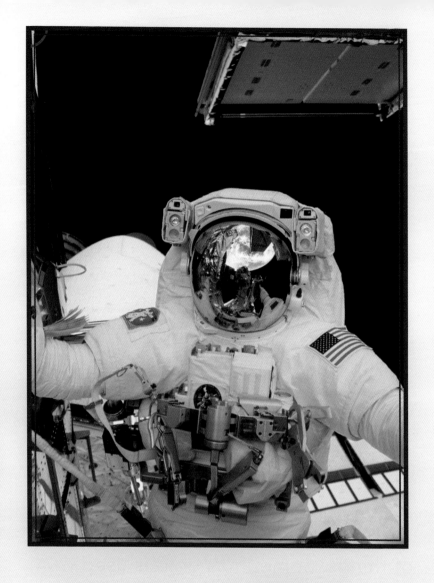

Gold is even used in space. Helmet visors are coated with gold to protect astronauts' eyes from the bright sun.

Sometimes gold is found in streams and rivers. People sort gold flakes from the gravel at the bottom of streams using special pans.

In the late 1840s, many people rushed to California to look for gold. A man called James W. Marshall found a gold nugget that had settled under the gravel in a river. When the news got around, people came from all over the world. They thought they would find gold.

Today, there are huge machines that can dig gold out of rock. The machines crush the rocks, and the gold is removed.

Most of the world's gold is found in South Africa. There are many big gold mines there.

People love gold jewelry and other things made of gold. If something is special, it is often called "golden". Now you know why!

Think Critically

1. Why do you think gold lasts a long time?

2. Where is the biggest collection of gold in the world and who owns it?

3. What are three facts that you learned about gold?

4. What happened in California after James W. Marshall found a gold nugget?

5. Which is your favorite gold object from the book? Why?

 Science

Make a List Make a list of other kinds of metals besides gold. List one or two things that each metal is used to make.

School-Home Connection Show a family member the cover of the book. Tell them what you learned about gold. Try to find something at home that is made from gold or has gold parts.